D1252532

People at Home

CONCEPTS IN SOCIAL SCIENCE

FREDERICK M. KING
Director of Instruction
Rochester, Minnesota

DOROTHY KENDALL BRACKEN
Director, The Reading Clinic
Southern Methodist University
Dallas, Texas

MARGARET A. SLOAN
Reading Consultant
Rochester Public Schools
Rochester, Minnesota

LAIDLAW BROTHERS · PUBLISHERS
A Division of Doubleday & Company, Inc.
RIVER FOREST, ILLINOIS

Palo Alto, California   Dallas, Texas   Atlanta, Georgia   Toronto, Canada

The LAIDLAW SOCIAL SCIENCE PROGRAM

PEOPLE AND THEIR NEEDS
Concepts in Social Science

PEOPLE AT HOME
Concepts in Social Science

FAMILIES AND SOCIAL NEEDS
Concepts in Social Science

COMMUNITIES AND SOCIAL NEEDS
Concepts in Social Science

REGIONS AND SOCIAL NEEDS
Concepts in Social Science

USING THE SOCIAL STUDIES
Concepts in Social Science

THE SOCIAL STUDIES AND OUR COUNTRY
Concepts in Social Science

THE SOCIAL STUDIES AND OUR WORLD
Concepts in Social Science

The artwork for this book was done by ROGER HERRINGTON STUDIOS.

Photographs used in this book were supplied by the following:

Appel Color Photography: 18 *center left*, 31 *top right*, 61 *left*.

Authenticated News International: 34 *bottom*, 35 *bottom left*, 42 *top*.

Bernadine Baily—'Round the World Photos: 20 *center left*, 91 *left*.

Dennis Brokaw from National Audubon Society: 55 *top*.

Chicago Department of Urban Renewal: 14 *top right*.

Charles Phelps Cushing: 19, 36 *bottom left*, 36 *right*, 61 *center*.

CustomCraft: 6-7 *top*, 7 *bottom left*, 15 *bottom right*, 20 *bottom left*, 24 *bottom left*, 24 *top left*, 27, 28 *top*, 30 *top left*, 32 *top left*, 37 *top left*, 37 *bottom left*, 38 *top right*, 39 *top*, 43 *top*, 43 *bottom*.

De Wys, Inc.: 4 *top*, 6 *bottom left*, 9 *left*, 9 *bottom*, 31 *bottom left*, 33, 40 *left*, 42 *bottom*, 47 *top left*, 63 *top*, 63 *top right*, 72 *right*, 89 *top*.

Ford Motor Company: 46 *top left*.

Harrison Forman World Travel, Inc.: 69 *bottom*, 70 *top left*, 70 *bottom left*, 70 *top right*, 71 *bottom right*, 72 *left*, 73 *top*, 73 *bottom right*, 74 *left*, 74 *top right*, 74 *bottom*, 77 *top*, 77 *center left*, 77 *bottom left*, 77 *bottom right*, 78 *bottom*, 79 *left*, 80 *top*, 82 *top left*, 82 *bottom center*, 83 *bottom right*, 90 *top*, 90 *bottom*.

John G. Gelinas, New York: 66 *bottom left*, 67, 74 *center right*, 79 *bottom right*, 82 *top right*, 83 *top left*, 90 *center*.

Grant Heilman: 14 *bottom*, 15 *bottom left*, 18 *top*, 18 *right*, 22, 30 *top right*, 30 *bottom left*, 30 *bottom right*, 37 *center left*, 50 *top*, 54, 61 *right*, 63 *left*.

Leon V. Kofod: 40 *right*, 66 *top left*, 68 *bottom*, 69 *top*, 71 *top right*, 72 *bottom left*, 73 *bottom left*, 75 *top left*, 76 *top*, 78 *top*, 79 *top right*, 80 *bottom*, 81.

Courtesy of *Ladies' Home Journal*: 25 *top left*.

Harold M. Lambert Studios: 12 *right*.

Cy La Tour: 92 *bottom left*, 92 *bottom right*.

Durango Mendoza/Tom Stack & Associates: 11 *top*, 11 *bottom right*, 40 *bottom right*.

J. M. Miller: 51 *top*.

Monkmeyer Press Photo Service: 12 *left*, 32 *top right*, 34 *top*, 42 *center*, 44 *top left*, 50 *bottom*, 64 *top right*, 70-71 *bottom*, 75 *bottom*, 82 *bottom left*, 93.

National Aeronautics Space Administration: 51 *bottom*.

Photo Trends, Inc.: 24 *bottom center*, 32 *bottom right*, 32 *bottom left*, 44 *top right*.

Publix: 9 *top*, 18 *bottom left*, 20 *top right*, 24 *top center*, 39 *bottom*, 45 *right*.

Donald Riedl: 10, 37 *right*, 43 *center*.

H. Armstrong Roberts: 4 *bottom*, 5, 7 *right*, 13 *bottom left*, 13 *top right*, 13 *bottom right*, 14 *top left*, 15 *top*, 20 *center right*, 24 *top right*, 28 *bottom*, 29, 31 *top left*, 31 *bottom right*, 35 *top*, 35 *bottom right*, 36 *top left*, 38 *left*, 38 *bottom right*, 41, 44 *bottom*, 45 *top left*, 45 *bottom left*, 46 *top center*, 46 *top right*, 48, 49 *top*, 52, 63 *bottom right*, 65 *top left*, 87, 89 *bottom*, 91 *right*.

Three Lions, Inc.: 71 *top left*, 75 *top right*, 92 *top left*.

Union Pacific Railroad Colorphoto: 49 *bottom*, 55 *bottom*.

Terry Wood: 11 *bottom left*, 92 *top right*.

Zentrale Farbbild Agentur: 13 *top left*, 13 *center right*, 63 *bottom*, 66 *bottom right*, 68 *top*, 76 *bottom*, 84.

ISBN-0-8445-6621-7

Copyright © 1974, 1972 by Laidlaw Brothers, Publishers

A Division of Doubleday & Company, Inc.

Printed in the United States of America

123456789   3210987654

UNIT
1   PEOPLE AND HOMES

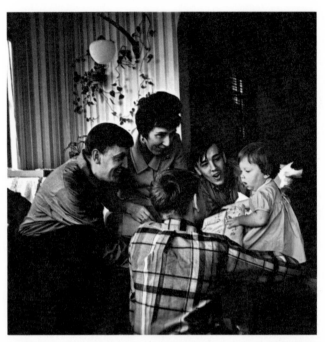

1. Families

What things do families need?

What things does your family need?

How does each person help in a family?

How do you help in your home?

Why do families have rules?

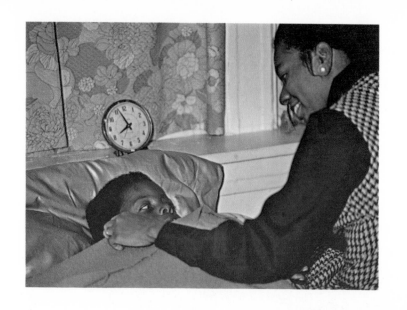

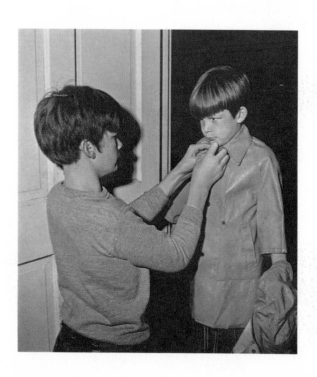

What rules does your family have?

What rights do people in families have?

What rights do you have?

2. Houses

JUST FOR FUN

Make a play house.

Use clay, cardboard, or a box.

What kinds of houses do you see here?

What kind of house do you live in?

What rooms does this house have?

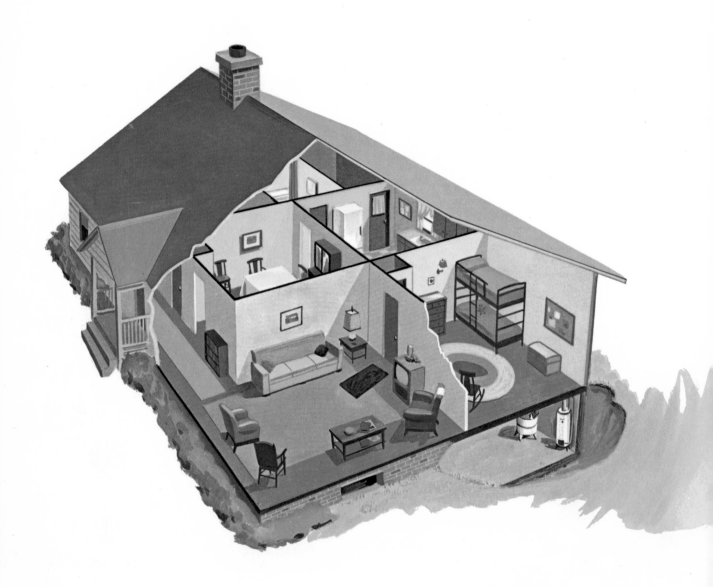

What rooms does your house have?

How do people go from room to room?

How do you go from room to room in your house?

What kinds of buildings do you see here?

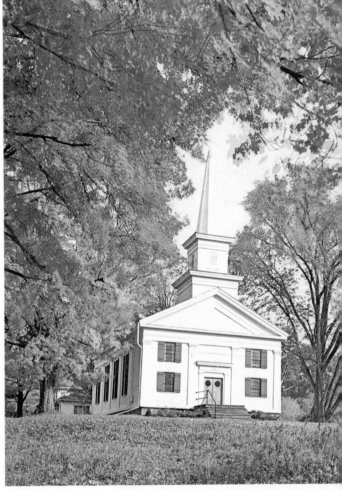

What buildings like these have you seen?

3. Streets

JUST FOR FUN

Make some streets on a sand table.

Put some play houses along the streets.

What are streets like?

What is your street like?

Who are the people on a street?

Who are the people on your street?

21

Where do streets go?

Where does your street go?

How do maps show where streets go?

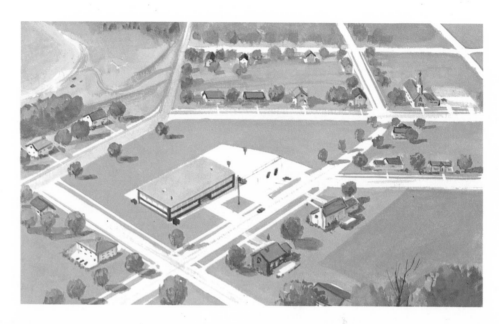

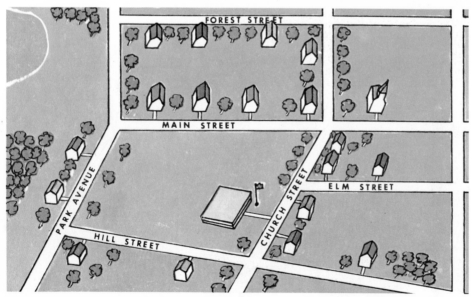

What streets do you follow to school?

Checkup Time

1. What do families need?

2. Where do families live?

3. Which map shows streets?

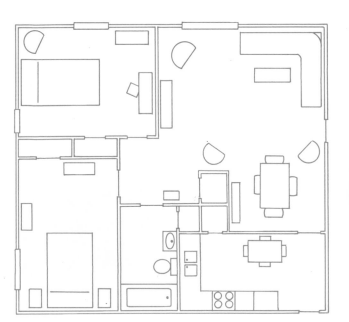

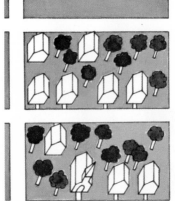

FIND OUT

What food do they like best?

Your family

Your mother's family

Were the answers the same? Why?

1. Helping One Another

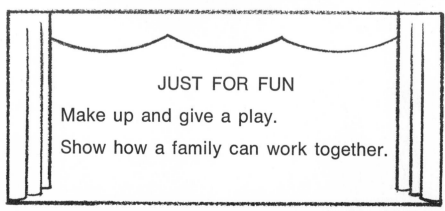

JUST FOR FUN

Make up and give a play.

Show how a family can work together.

How do people in a family help each other?

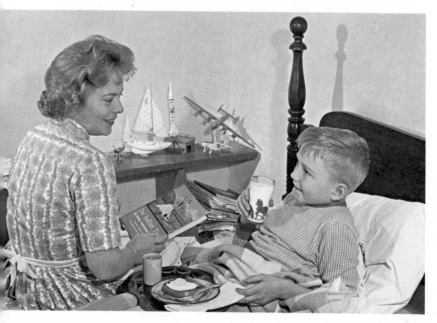

How do you help others in your family?

How do workers far away help families?

How do workers far away help you?

How do workers in your town help your family?

What workers in your town help you?

2. Family Money

JUST FOR FUN

Make a list of things a family has to buy.

What jobs do fathers have?

What job does your father do away from home?

What jobs do fathers do at home?

What jobs does your father do at home?

What jobs do mothers do at home?

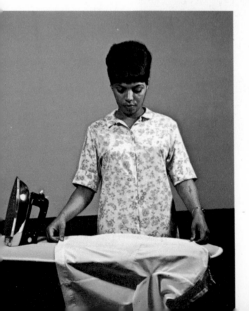

What jobs does your mother do at home?

What jobs do mothers do away from home?

What other jobs do mothers have away from home?

What jobs do children do at home?

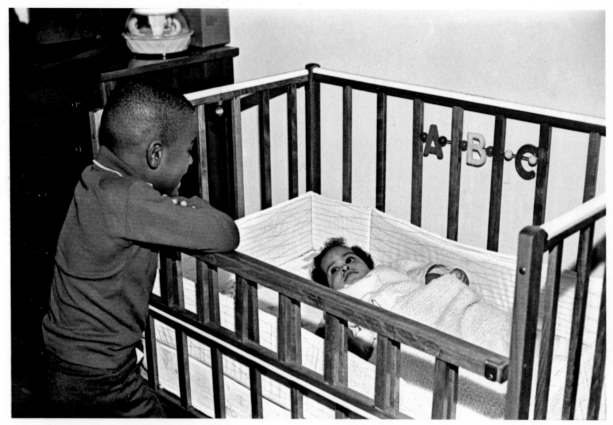

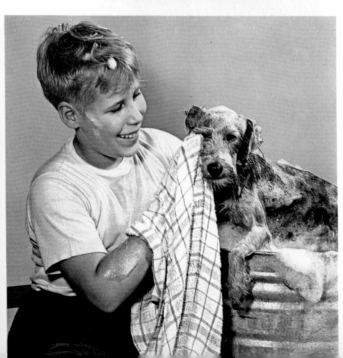

What jobs do you do at home?

How can children help to save money?

How do you help to save money?

3. Spending Money

Who pays for these things?

What things does your family pay for?

Which of these things cost money?

How does your family have fun?

Checkup Time

1. What jobs do fathers do away from home?

2. How can children help to save money?

46

3. What two things do mothers do at home?

 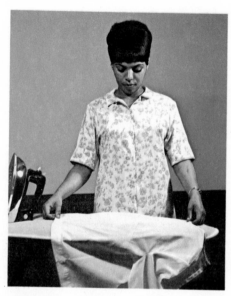 

FIND OUT
What things have wheels?

Which can you use to do work?

Which can you use to have fun?

Which cost a dollar or less?

GLOBES AND MAPS

1. How the Earth Looks

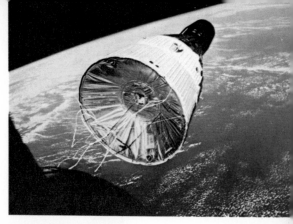

JUST FOR FUN

Find pictures of the earth from space.

Talk about them.

How does the earth look from near by?

How much of the earth can you see?

How does the earth look from far away?

How much of the earth could you see from the moon?

Why is a globe a good map of the earth?

What do you know about globes?

2. Using a Globe

JUST FOR FUN

Make a little cutout.

Have it stand for you.

Put it on a globe where you live.

How can you find land on a globe?

On which body of land do you live?

How can you find water on a globe?

Do you see more land or water on a globe?

Where do these boys live?

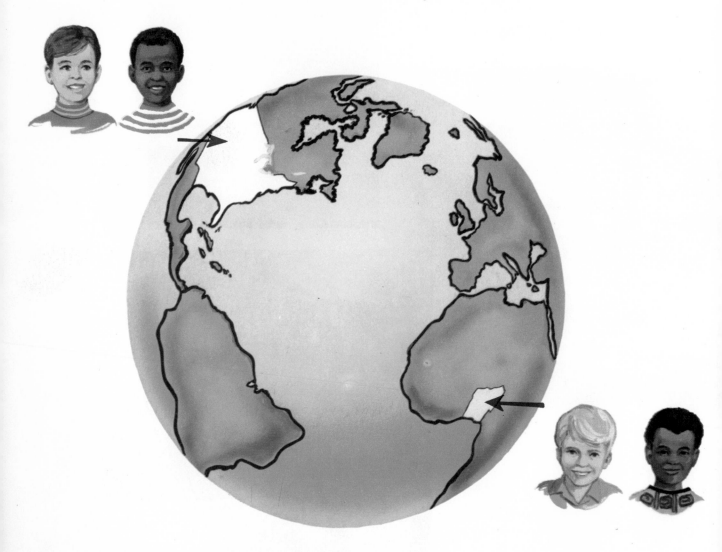

In what country do you live?

3. Using Maps

How did the children make this map?

How could you make a map?

How can you tell which way is north?

Why does a map show north, south, east, and west?

How is a map like a picture?

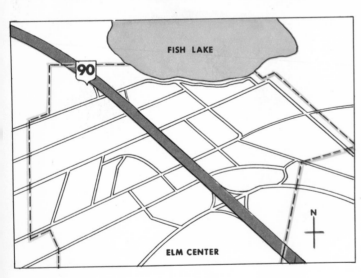

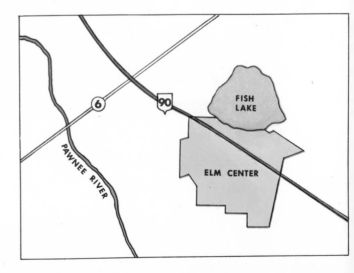

How can you use maps?

What kinds of places do you see on this map?

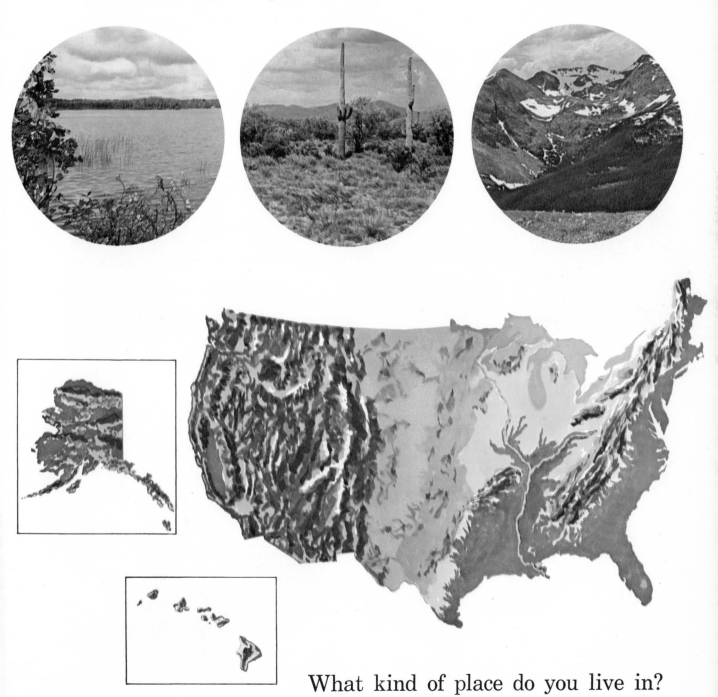

What kind of place do you live in?

What places do you see on this map?

What faraway places have you seen?

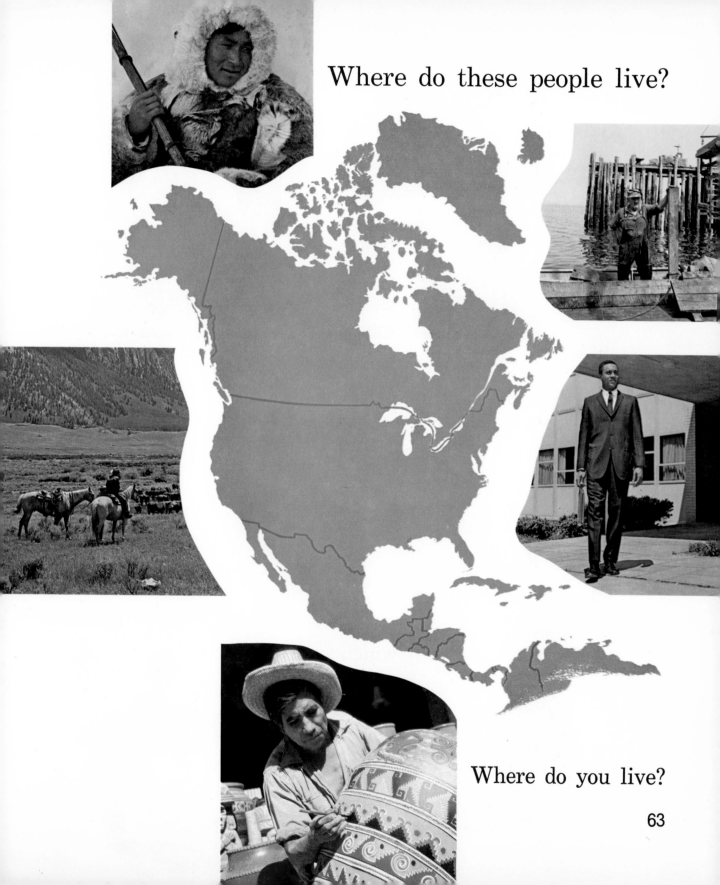

Where do these people live?

Where do you live?

Checkup Time

1. Why is a globe a good map?

2. What do these maps show?

3. How can you tell which way is north?

4. Which map shows land and water?

FIND OUT

Is your state on a map?

Is your city on a map?

Is your city on a globe?

66

1. Families

JUST FOR FUN

Find pictures of families in faraway places.

How are these families like yours?

What do these families need?

How are the people like you?

What jobs do fathers have?

Which jobs are like jobs in your city?

What jobs do mothers have?

What does your mother do that African mothers do?

2. How the People Live

JUST FOR FUN

Find pictures of homes in faraway places.

How are these homes like yours?

What are the houses like?

How is your house different from these houses?

What are the streets like?

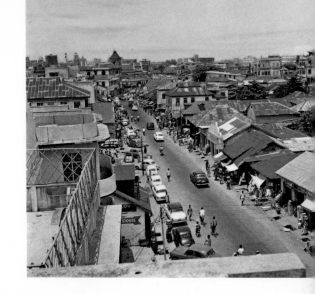

Which street is most like your street?

How do the people travel?

In which of these ways could you travel?

How has living changed?

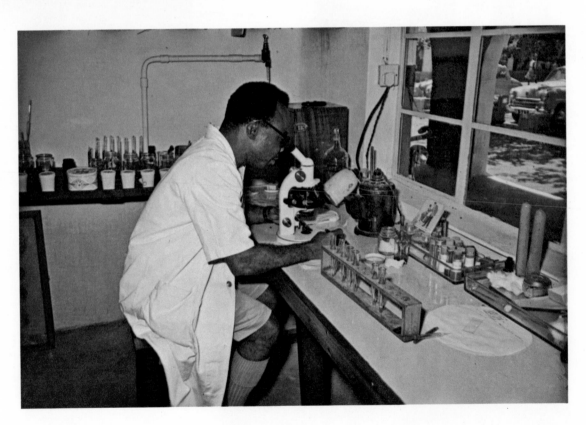

How might our country change?

3. Children

JUST FOR FUN

Find someone who has gone to a faraway land.

Ask him about the children there.

What do the children do in school?

How is your school like these?

How do the children have fun?

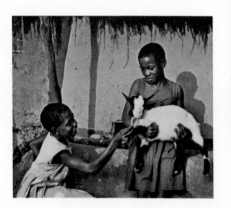

How are these children like you?

Checkup Time

1. What do families in West Africa need?

2. What do people in West Africa do?

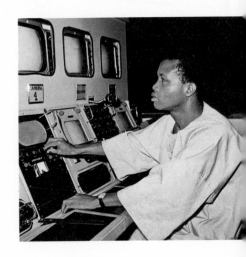

3. Which three pictures were taken in West Africa?

FIND OUT

Can you carry these on your head?

A big box   A big basket

How big a load can you carry?

On your head   In your arms

OUR COUNTRY

1. Holidays

FEBRUARY

SUN	MON	TUE	WED	THU	FRI	SAT
						1
2	3	4	5	6	7	8
9	10	11	12	13	14	15
16	17	18	19	20	21	22
23	24	25	26	27	28	

JUST FOR FUN

Find or make a calendar.

Put a circle around each holiday.

Why do we have Thanksgiving?

What do you do on Thanksgiving Day?

Why do we have Columbus Day?

What do you do on Columbus Day?

Why do we have Independence Day?

What do you do on Independence Day?

What do people in West Africa do on holidays?

How are holidays in West Africa like ours?

2. The Flag

JUST FOR FUN

Draw our flag. Use the right colors.

Use the right number of stars.

Use the right number of stripes.

How do we honor our flag?

Where have you seen the flag flying?

Why do we pledge allegiance to the flag?

What does "pledge allegiance" mean to you?

Checkup Time

1. What events took place on these days?

JULY

SUN	MON	TUE	WED	THU	FRI	SAT
		1	2	3	4	5
6	7	8	9	10	11	12
13	14	15	16	17	18	19
20	21	22	23	24	25	26
27	28	29	30	31		

OCTOBER

SUN	MON	TUE	WED	THU	FRI	SAT
			1	2	3	4
5	6	7	8	9	10	11
12	13	14	15	16	17	18
19	20	21	22	23	24	25
26	27	28	29	30	31	

2. What are these children doing?

3. Which pictures show holidays in our country?

FIND OUT

What holiday do they like best?

A friend   Your mother

Your grandmother

Were the answers the same? Why?

KEY SOCIAL SCIENCE WORDS

Certain words in this text provide clues to a large cluster of key ideas (concepts) in one or more of the social science disciplines. These are the words listed below. The page references are to pages where one or more ideas in each idea cluster are presented.

ANTHROPOLOGY AND SOCIOLOGY

Clothing, 6-7, 66, 68-69, 79

Families, 5, 6-7, 8-9, 10-11, 12, 27, 28-29, 33, 36, 37, 38, 39, 40, 41, 42-43, 48, 67, 86-87

Fathers, 34, 36, 70-71

Food, 6-7, 68-69, 73

Fun, 44-45, 81

Homes, 4, 6-7

Houses, 4, 6-7, 13, 14-15, 16-17, 20, 68-69, 74

Mothers, 37, 38, 72

People, 4, 21, 63, 66

Rights, 10-11, 12

Rules, 10-11

School, 80

Streets, 19, 20, 75

ECONOMICS

Cost, 41, 44-45

Jobs, 21, 26, 33, 34-35, 36, 37, 38, 70-71, 72

Money, 40, 41, 44-45

Needs, 41, 42-43

Pay, 41, 42-43

Save, 40

Spend, 41

Wants, 44-45

Work, 26, 27, 28-29, 33, 34-35, 36, 37, 38, 39, 70-71, 72

Workers, 26, 30-31, 32, 70-71

GEOGRAPHY

Country, 62, 63

Desert, 61

Earth, 49, 50, 51, 52

East, 59

Globe, 52, 53, 54, 55, 62

Lake, 60, 61

Land, 54

Map, 23, 48, 57, 58, 59, 60

Mountain, 61

North, 59

South, 59

Streets, 22-23, 57, 58

Water, 55

West, 59

HISTORY AND POLITICAL SCIENCE

Change, 78

Columbus Day, 85, 88

Country, 84

Flag, 91, 92, 93

Holidays, 85, 90

Honor, 92

Independence Day, 85, 89

Map, 62

Pledge of Allegiance, 93

Rights, 11, 12

Rules, 10-11

Thanksgiving, 85, 86-87